PHILADELPHIA ICONS

PHILADELPHIA ICONS

50 CLASSIC VIEWS
OF THE CITY OF BROTHERLY LOVE

Karen Ivory

Guilford, Connecticut

Project editor: David Legere
Text design: Casey Shain

Library of Congress Cataloging-in-Publication Data
Ivory, Karen.
  Philadelphia icons : 50 classic views of the City of Brotherly Love / Karen Ivory.
    p. cm.
  ISBN 978-0-7627-6031-2
  1. Philadelphia (Pa.)—Pictorial works. 2. Philadelphia (Pa.)—Description and travel. I. Title.
  F158.37.I95 2011
  974.8'11—dc22
                                                                        2010034472

Printed in China

10 9 8 7 6 5 4 3 2 1

CONTENTS

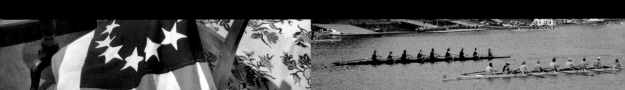

INTRODUCTION

The first thing that I learned when I started to think about writing a book on Philadelphia icons is *not* to ask anyone from Philadelphia about what *they* think are Philadelphia icons. Philly takes its hometown treasures very seriously. I started brainstorming a list of about seventy, but after soliciting the opinions of friends and colleagues, that list mushroomed to more than a hundred. Sorry, folks—I could only include fifty. Editor's orders.

I admit to being a little sneaky and integrating would-be icons on their own into another entry in some cases—see, for example, Rocky and "Yo." (How would I have photographed "Yo" anyway?) But some icons are going to have to wait for the sequel, while others ended up on the trash heap. Several homegrown Philadelphians, being slightly prone to sarcasm, suggested as icons the oil refinery tanks and scrap metal mountains that dominate the landscape near the airport. There were numerous nominations for the Schuylkill Expressway and other beloved, bumper-to-bumper thoroughfares. The Parking Authority, the City Wage Tax . . . Sure, there are things to gripe about

in any city, but in the end it's hard not to put a positive spin on things in Philadelphia, though we don't often like to admit it.

Full disclosure: I wasn't raised in Philadelphia and freely admit that despite having lived here for more than twenty-five years, I may not qualify as a true Philadelphian. However, I would argue that the outsider status allows me to recognize some of the city's special, albeit a little quirky, attributes, whereas "lifers" take everything for granted.

Philadelphia is, without question, a city of icons. From its iconic "City of Brotherly Love" motto to the symbols of our nation's democracy, the city is replete with images that resonate deeply in the psyche of its citizens, if not the country. And while some of our homegrown traditions have been exported throughout the country or even the world, there is no doubt about what constitutes "the real thing." Have you had a good cheesesteak in Tokyo lately? (And my apologies to those institutions and spell-check creators who think "cheesesteak" should be two words. Not in my Philly.)

Philadelphia's tourist mavens like to point visitors to "America's most historic mile," which does indeed contain a wealth of iconic images. Turn around or cross the street and there's another one. But I hope this book offers an impetus to break the boundaries of the historic district and discover some of the other iconic people, places, and things that make Philly the unique city it is.

PHILADELPHIA ICONS

30TH STREET STATION

They just don't make 'em like they used to. Philadelphia's regal 30th Street Station has been welcoming train passengers in style since the 1930s. Riding up the escalator from the tracks below, visitors ascend into a soaring space that harkens back to the glory days of train travel.

Designed by Graham, Anderson, Probst & White, the neoclassical building remains the largest active rail station in the country, and among the most majestic. The exterior is marked by seventy-one-foot-high Corinthian columns, the interior by its ornate bas-relief ceiling and art deco chandeliers. Near the east entrance a prominent bronze statue depicting the archangel Michael lifting the body of a soldier honors Pennsylvania Railroad employees killed in World War II. Movie buffs will recognize the statue from the opening scenes of the 1985 movie *Witness*. The station also played a supporting role in *Trading Places* and hometown-boy-made-good M. Night Shyamalan's *Unbreakable*. The cavernous main room has also been put to other good uses, serving as a venue for weddings,

30th and Market Streets Philadelphia, PA 19019

parties, and even dance performances highlighting the building's windowed walkways.

When it was built, 30th Street Station featured several new innovations, including a pneumatic tube system and an electronic intercom. The roof was reinforced with concrete to allow a landing space for small aircraft, though that plan was wisely never carried out. Even more odd, perhaps, the original design also included a chapel, a mortuary, and more than three thousand square feet of hospital space. Those spaces have long since given way to more traditional uses, like office space, fast food, and quick coffee.

For decades there was much debate about what to do with the parking deck built over the tracks as they enter the station. Lofty schemes included such proposals as building a new city hall or a new sports stadium, or placing the convention center there. In the end commerce won out, and 2005 saw the construction next door of César Pelli's Cira Centre, giving the 30th Street Station some competition in the architectural drama department.

ACADEMY OF MUSIC

Affectionately known as the Grand Old Lady of Broad Street, the Academy of Music is Philadelphia's most cherished performing arts space—no offense to the newer and flashier Kimmel Center down the street. When you've been around since 1875, you garner some hard-core fans. Built in 1857, the academy was home to the renowned Philadelphia Orchestra for more than a hundred years. Once the orchestra headed off to the state-of-the-art acoustics at the Kimmel, the Academy of Music underwent a major renovation and now serves as home base for the Opera Company of Philadelphia and the Pennsylvania Ballet, as well as host to traveling Broadway productions. It is the oldest opera hall in the country still used for its original purpose.

Its elegant yet simple brick exterior is still lit by flickering gaslights; Philadelphia architects Napoleon LeBrun and Gustavus Runge anticipated that at a later date, marble facing would be added. The stunning interior was designed with the La Scala Opera House in Milan in mind, its intricately painted ceiling illuminated by a five-

Broad and Locust Streets Philadelphia, PA 19104 (215) 893-1999 www.academy ofmusic.org

thousand-pound crystal chandelier. The chandelier was removed from the academy for the first time in 2007 and sent to southern France for a thirteen-month restoration project. When it was originally installed, it took four hours and twelve workers to lower the chandelier; now it practically flies down in five minutes for its annual cleaning thanks to a fancy new hoisting system.

Over the years the Academy of Music has hosted a who's who of the world's top performing artists and set the stage for numerous worldwide premieres. Leopold Stokowski, who had a long, prestigious association with the Philadelphia Orchestra, conducted the American premiere of Mahler's Eighth Symphony at the academy in 1916.

The academy is also noted for a few nonmusical traditions. Its ushers, decked out in burgundy jackets and bow ties, are said to be among the best in the world. And each January one of the most lavish events of the city's social calendar, the Academy Ball, draws a who's who from the society pages in all their finery to the building's beloved ballroom.

ART MUSEUM

Perched regally on high, the Philadelphia Museum of Art both provides and is one of the best views in town, gazing down toward City Hall and keeping watch over the cultural gems on the Ben Franklin Parkway. It can be hard to decide whether to stand at the top of the steps and take in the view or turn around and take in the treasures that lie inside.

The building's chief designer was Horace Trumbauer & Associates' Julian Abele, the first major African-American architect in the United States, who drew his inspiration from Greek temples.

Particularly noteworthy are the museum's American collections, highlighted by a strong collection of Philadelphia-made furniture and silver and rural Pennsylvania furniture and crafts. Also significant is its collection of paintings by Thomas Eakins, Philadelphia's best-known hometown artist. The museum, along with the Pennsylvania Academy of Fine Arts, was instrumental in keeping Eakins's masterpiece, *The Gross Clinic,* in Philadelphia when Thomas Jefferson University put it up for sale in 1996.

2600 Benjamin Franklin Parkway Philadelphia, PA 19130 (215) 763-8100 www.phila museum.org

The modern art collection contains particularly impressive works by Pablo Picasso, Marcel Duchamp, and Constantin Brancusi. At the top of the magnificent Great Stair Hall, with its Augustus Saint-Gaudens *Diana* weathervane, are galleries containing one of the world's greatest collections of arms and armor. The Great Hall itself has become a destination for the younger crowd on selected Friday nights, when the museum kicks back, stays open late, and offers food, drinks, and an eclectic mix of music and dance performances.

The museum is currently executing a ten-year master plan that will more than double its public space. Architect Frank Gehry is in charge, but don't look for a dramatic building. The eighty-thousand-square-foot addition is being built entirely underground, leaving the famous Greek Revival facade untouched. The first phase of the expansion project involved the renovation of the art deco former headquarters of the Fidelity Mutual Life Insurance Company across the street.

BARNES FOUNDATION

For a long time you could say the Barnes Foundation was the most important cultural institution in Philadelphia that hardly anyone had heard of. Tucked away on a small, tree-lined suburban street, one of the world's greatest collections of art lived out its bizarre existence without much notice. Art aficionados from the world over would make pilgrimages to visit the unique collection, but Philadelphians were mostly oblivious. Not any more. As of 2012, after a prolonged, complicated run of court cases, the Barnes Foundation will take its place on the Ben Franklin Parkway among the city's other treasured museums.

This is no ordinary museum. The amazing collection was the creation of the eccentric Albert Barnes, a physician who made a fortune after developing an early treatment for eye infections. He spent the rest of his life accumulating art and developing his foundation's educational mission. He never intended his galleries to be open to the public and was often at odds with Philadelphia's established art community.

The collection is now valued at around $25 billion and includes

20th Street and Benjamin Franklin Parkway Philadelphia, PA 19103 www.barnes foundation.org

some 181 Renoirs, 69 Cézannes, and 59 Matisses. The works are displayed exactly in the idiosyncratic way Barnes specified—symmetrical groupings organized around specific themes that mostly elude visitors. The paintings aren't identified, except on laminated handouts. A little-known van Gogh is tucked in the corner next to a painting by an obscure artist. The paintings are interspersed with intricate pieces of ironwork, Pennsylvania Dutch folk art, and African sculptures, among other things. An indenture set up by Barnes stipulated it must always be so.

After Barnes's death in 1951, the squabbling began and the courts intervened to allow limited public access to the collection. Over the years the foundation's trustees slowly chipped away at Barnes's indenture, and in the 1990s the Orphans Court ruled that the collection could be moved to the far more accessible site on the Parkway. The new building, designed by New York architects Tod Williams and Billie Tsien, replicates the original galleries so the collection is still displayed exactly as Barnes intended.

BENJAMIN FRANKLIN

"Founding father" hardly covers it—this guy did it all. He was a scientist, a printer, a postmaster, a satirist, a musician, an economist, a statesman, and a philosopher. He invented bifocal glasses, the Franklin stove, the odometer, medical devices, a glass musical instrument, swim fins—and, okay, even though he didn't actually "invent" electricity, he did come up with the lightning rod. He published a newspaper. He founded a fire company and the nation's first fire insurance company. He created the first public lending library. He got the ball rolling on the University of Pennsylvania. He negotiated peace treaties. And, oh yeah, he helped write the Declaration of Independence and the Constitution. He was Benjamin Franklin, sometimes known as "the President of the United States who never was President of the United States."

Franklin's adventures in Philadelphia started by breaking the law, when he ran away from his Boston family as a sixteen-year-old. But by then Puritan values were in his blood, and at the ripe old age of twenty, he developed a

list of thirteen virtues to cultivate his character: temperance, silence, order, resolution, frugality, industry, sincerity, justice, moderation, cleanliness, tranquility, chastity, and humility. Virtues notwithstanding, he was also known to enjoy a Poor Richard's Ale at the Crooked Billet Inn and is credited with the saying "Beer is living proof that God loves us and wants us to be happy."

Franklin's lifetime of achievement (1706-1790) earned his image a place on coins and dollar bills, and his name is all over the map, with endless towns, counties, and schools named in his honor. Similarly, his name and face crop up constantly in Philadelphia. He is duly memorialized at the University of Pennsylvania and the Franklin Institute science museum. There's the bridge and the parkway. And, despite Franklin's famous thriftiness, his image looks down over his namesake Franklin Mills Shopping Mall in Northeast Philadelphia, a huge outlet shopping center that at one point was the most visited tourist attraction in Pennsylvania, a depressing statistic if ever there was one.

BETSY ROSS

The legend of Betsy Ross as the seamstress of the nation's first flag may or may not be 100 percent historically accurate, but because we're talking icons here, let's go with it. The story of the flag was put forth by her grandson years after her death, but many historians believe there's enough evidence to support it. What is undeniable is that Ross's life provides a fascinating glimpse into the life of a working-class woman in colonial Philadelphia.

Born Elisabeth Griscom in 1752, the eighth of seventeen children, Betsy became an accomplished upholsterer at a young age. Over the years she would be widowed three times but because of her skills as a seamstress was able to support herself and her seven children.

In May 1777 Betsy was running a successful upholstery business she had started with her first husband, John Ross. After John's death, she earned extra money by mending uniforms and making tents for the Continental army. The story goes that three men— George Washington, Robert Morris,

Betsy Ross House
239 Arch Street
Philadelphia, PA
19106
(215) 686-1252
www.betsyross house.org

and George Ross (John Ross's uncle)— arrived in Betsy's shop with a sketch of a flag bearing thirteen red and white stripes and thirteen six-pointed stars. They wanted to know, could she make a flag from the design? Then, with one snip of her scissors, Betsy suggested they make the stars more attractive by using only five points, and all agreed. That same year Congress adopted the Stars and Stripes as the national flag.

Betsy would outlive her second and third husbands and, with her daughter, Clarissa, kept her upholstery and flag-making business going strong. She didn't quit working until she was seventy-six years old and going blind; she died in 1836 at the age of eighty-four.

Today the house where Betsy Ross lived from 1773 to 1785 is filled with period furnishings, some of which belonged to Ross herself. Visitors can see a variety of Ross's belongings, including her eyeglasses and Bible, as well as the room from which she ran her upholstery business.

BOATHOUSE ROW

It's one of Philadelphia's premier postcard shots: Boathouse Row, a line of ten charming Victorian structures, outlined in small lights at night, proudly standing sentinel over the city's revered rowing history.

The houses—each with its own storied history—are home base for the city's rowing clubs. They awake early, as individuals and teams arrive at dawn to get in a workout on the river before the work or school day begins. The doors open and out come the slender, sleek sculls, which are soon propelled through the waters of the Schuylkill by rowers working in complete unison.

It was the construction of the Fairmount Dam in 1821 that created ideal conditions for rowing on the Schuylkill, and it didn't take long for word to spread. The first recorded regatta on the river, between the Blue Devils and Imps barge clubs, was held in 1835. The river's wide, mile-and-a-quarter course is now home to more regattas than any other U.S. city, including two of the nation's largest: the Dad Vail collegiate regatta and the Stotesbury Cup high school regatta, which bring thousands of fans to the Schuylkill's shores each May. The city's annual Dragon Boat Festival grows more popular each year.

The Schuylkill course has produced a long roster of rowing champions, including the Kelly family for whom Kelly Drive is named: Jack Kelly, whose daughter Grace went on to some fame of her own, and his son John Kelly Jr., a four-time Olympian.

Boathouse Row had seen better days by the 1970s, when Philadelphia lighting designer Raymond Grenald came up with the idea to increase the houses' visibility by outlining the architectural frames and portals in small lights. The project was an instant hit, as the warm lights were reflected in the waters of the Schuylkill. A 2005 upgrade to a new, not-quite-so-warm LED-based lighting system saves the city about $57,000 a year in lightbulbs and energy costs and allows for color changes when the spirit moves.

THE CALDER FAMILY

They've been called Philadelphia's "First Family of Sculpture"—the Calders: three generations of artists who are responsible for some of the city's most iconic sculptural statements.

In the beginning there was Alexander Milne Calder. The son of a Scottish tombstone carver, he settled in Philadelphia in 1868 and studied with famed Philadelphia artist Thomas Eakins at the Pennsylvania Academy of the Fine Arts. Just five years later, Calder was commissioned to come up with models for City Hall. Did he ever. Over the next twenty years, he produced more than 250 marble and bronze sculptures that adorn the building, including his crowning achievement—the thirty-seven-foot-tall bronze of William Penn that sits atop the tower.

Next in line was son Alexander Stirling Calder, also a product of the Pennsylvania Academy of the Fine Arts, who assisted his father with the City Hall works as a young man. After a stint in Paris, Calder returned to Philadelphia, where he is best known as the genius behind the city's beloved Swann Memorial Fountain in Logan Square, just down the Parkway from City Hall. The fountain's three large Native American figures represent Philly's major local waterways—the Delaware River, the Schuylkill, and Wissahickon Creek—and are playfully joined by frogs, turtles, and two swans—a nod to Dr. Wilson Cary Swann, founder of the Philadelphia Fountain Society, for whom the fountain is named. Each spring the fountain is the scene of a long-standing tradition of the nearby Hallahan Catholic Girls High, whose uniformed students commemorate the end of the school year by jumping into the fountain en masse.

The third-generation Calder—also an Alexander—is represented at the Philadelphia Museum of Art by one of the modern mobiles for which he became famous. The mobile, *Ghost,* hangs in the Great Stair Hall of the museum, from which one can look out the doors down the Parkway, taking in works by the three generations of Calder men.

CHEESESTEAK

Philadelphians traveling anywhere outside the city will inevitably scoff when they come upon a restaurant's menu touting "Philly Cheesesteak." Come on. Why even bother? If you want a Philly cheesesteak, you have to be in Philly. Duh.

And not everyone does want one. Let's face it, the cheesesteak is basically a heart attack waiting to happen on a roll: piles of thinly sliced beef topped with mounds of cheese or, for some purists, processed Cheez Whiz. Still, there's no denying the cheesesteak is the city's signature sandwich.

The consensus is that this epic creation was invented in 1930 by Pasquale "Pat" Olivieri, who dubbed himself the "King of Steaks." Legend has it that Olivieri, a hot dog vendor, wanted something different for lunch one day, so he got some chopped meat from a butcher in the Italian Market, grilled it up on his hot dog grill with some onions, then slapped it on an Italian roll. A loyal cab driver customer pulled up just as Pat was chowing down, said

he'd like one too, and then said, "Forget the dogs, you should sell these." When the cabbie asked what he called his creation, Pat replied, "I guess you call it a steak." Voilà!

While there's agreement on the history, that's about where it ends. What's the best cheesesteak place in town? Wid or widout (onions, that is)? Cheez Whiz, provolone, or American? What's the appropriate roll? Peppers or no? If yes, hot or sweet? All subjects of great debate and the source of endless annual contests and surveys. Then there's the longstanding duel between Pat's (still run by the Olivieri family) and Geno's, the two South Philly standards that square off catercorner to each other at Ninth and Passyunk. Meanwhile, some swear by Jim's on South Street.

Wherever, it's best to be well prepared. Lots of napkins are critical until you perfect the Philly stance of leaning slightly forward so the grease—yes, there's usually lots of grease (remember, no one said this was healthy)—doesn't end up on your shirt.

CHINATOWN

In 1860 a man named Lee Fong opened a small Chinese laundry at the corner of Ninth and Race Streets; ten years later a restaurant called Mei-Hsian Lou followed suit nearby—the beginning of what would become Philadelphia's Chinatown. Though sometimes seemingly dwarfed by the enormous Pennsylvania Convention Center, the streets of Chinatown are filled with more than fifty restaurants as well as Chinese bakeries, gift shops, and grocery stores offering large selections of specialty noodles, hot sauces, and even buckets of live frogs and eels, if such things suit your fancy.

Between Vine and Race Streets, Eighth and Eleventh Streets

If you want Chinese food when you're in Philly, this is where you head. Philadelphians frequently argue about which is their favorite Chinatown restaurant. Today, in addition to Szechuan, Mandarin, and Hunan, visitors can dine at other ethnic restaurants as well—from Vietnamese to Burmese to Japanese.

Confined to a small area of just six square blocks, the close-knit residents of Chinatown have had to advocate for their community over the years, as the Vine Street Expressway and the convention center encroached. They successfully fought off efforts by developers to build a casino nearby, as well as a far-fetched idea a decade ago to build the city's new baseball stadium there.

Standing proud over Chinatown is the Friendship Gate, an ornate, brightly colored arch that celebrates the cultural exchange and friendship between Philadelphia and its sister city, Tianjin, in China. Completed in 1984, the forty-foot-structure is the first authentic Chinese gate built in the United States by artisans from China. Workers used traditional color combinations to detail the mythical creatures that scale the arch: the phoenix bringing good luck, and the dragon protecting the community from fire. Within the last decade the gate was completely repainted and brought back to its original luster by artists who came from Tianjin and worked with the local community.

CHRIST CHURCH AND GRAVEYARD

Among the many beautiful churches in Philadelphia, Christ Church exudes the most history. Visitors to the sanctuary can sit in the very pews occupied long ago by George Washington, Benjamin Franklin, and Betsy Ross. The same eight bells that rang out the news of the country's independence in 1776 still chime today. Historian David McCullough has written, "No other church has played a more significant role in our nation's birth."

The church was founded by members of the Church of England in 1695, a condition of William Penn's charter, with the construction of a small wooden structure. The six-hundred-year-old baptismal font used to baptize William Penn as a boy in England arrived from London's All Hallow Church in 1697. The current building was constructed between 1727 and 1744. Benjamin Franklin himself organized a lottery to raise the money for the tower and the steeple, which was

20 North American Street Philadelphia, PA 19106 (215) 922-1695 www.oldchrist church.org

added in 1754 and qualified the church as the tallest building in the United States until 1865. The pulpit was built by John Folwell, the same craftsman who made the "Rising Sun" chair used by George Washington in Independence Hall. The elegant, understated sanctuary and the classic symmetrical facade make Christ Church one of the most striking examples of Georgian Colonial architecture in the country.

Equally as interesting as the church itself are its burial grounds a short walk away at Fifth and Arch Streets. Christ Church acquired the grounds in 1719 at what was the considered "the outskirts of town." Seven signers of the Declaration of Independence and five signers of the Constitution are buried here. By far the most visited grave is Ben Franklin's. Ben is buried with his wife, Deborah, under a stone that is almost always covered with pennies left by visitors who still remember Franklin's credo: "A penny saved is a penny earned."

CITY HALL

There is little doubt about which iconic image stands at the very heart of Philadelphia. It's hard to miss City Hall, its commanding presence towering over the place where Broad and Market come together, smack in the center of downtown. The tallest masonry building in the world, City Hall took thirty years to build. When it was finished in 1901, it fulfilled one of William Penn's original visions for the city: He had always intended for the city's Center Square to be used for "publik concerns."

This Second Empire beauty was designed by John McArthur Jr. The first floor is built of solid granite, the walls twenty-two feet thick in some places. More than 250 sculptures adorn the exterior, all by Alexander Milne Calder, who also designed the bronze likeness of William Penn that rises five hundred feet above the street. The thirty-seven-foot-tall Penn is the largest sculpture on a building anywhere. For years there was a gentleman's agreement between city planners and developers that no building in Philadelphia could be taller than the top of Penn's

Broad and Market Streets Philadelphia, PA 19107 (215) 686-2840

hat. That held until One Liberty Place opened in 1987, and there are those who believe the lackluster performance of the city's sports teams since then can be blamed on the change—the so-called "curse of William Penn" (with the notable exception of the 2008 Phillies' World Series win).

City Hall hasn't always been universally loved. Louis Kahn, Philadelphia's famed modernist architect, dubbed it "the most disreputable and disrespected building in Philadelphia." Some city leaders in the 1950s even proposed tearing it down. Luckily they didn't, because the American Institute of Architects later called the building "perhaps the greatest single effort of late nineteenth-century architecture."

Lest you think those behind the recent renovation of the tower were color-blind, the lighter color was actually called for in the original design, with the thought it would make the statue of Penn appear more prominent. The tower is open for tours; its observation deck provides the only publicly accessible panoramic views of the city.

THE CLOTHESPIN

Philadelphia's "One Percent" for Art" program, which rewards developers for including public art in their projects, has resulted in a lot of art in the city, some of it more loved than others. There's no question that one of the most notable—and hotly debated— is the forty-five-foot-tall clothespin that rises in front of an office building at 15th and Market.

Claes Oldenburg's 1976 sculpture has been commanding its Center City corner for so long that most Philadelphians pass by without noticing. But visitors can't help but do a double take. Corten steel "legs," turned rusty brown over the years, swoop up to form a stylized version of a clothespin, a trademark classic in Oldenburg's oeuvre of huge everyday objects. (His *Split Button* resides in front of the library at the University of Pennsylvania.) Oldenburg himself compared his clothespin to *The Kiss*—a famous Brancusi sculpture in the Philadelphia Museum of Art, where two separate forms come together in an embrace.

15th and Market Streets Philadelphia

Many believe the clothespin sculpture is a humorous nod to the adjacent tower of City Hall. Some see the number 76, which happens to be the year the sculpture was installed, in time for the country's bicentennial. Coincidence?

The story goes that Oldenburg came up with the idea for the clothespin on an airplane flight into Chicago. He was traveling with a clothespin, ostensibly because he liked the shape. As he looked out the window at Chicago's downtown skyscrapers, it occurred to him that from his aerial vantage point, the buildings appeared to be the same size as his clothespin.

Love it or hate it—and there are plenty on both sides—there's no doubt the sleek sculpture provides quite the contrast to the ornamentation overload across the street at City Hall. And now, the clothespin is being joined by another Oldenburg creation—this time a giant paintbrush that extends over a plaza at the Academy of Fine Arts on Broad Street.

COMCAST CENTER

If something has to have been around a long time to be considered iconic, then the Comcast Center doesn't qualify. But being the tallest building in Philly, it's hard to miss and there's no question it dramatically changed the city skyline.

One of a few major corporations headquartered in Philadelphia, Comcast comes by its sturdy stature honestly. The company is now the country's largest provider of cable services and, with its intended purchase of NBC Universal, would be a major player in programming as well. Comcast occupies almost 90 percent of the fifty-eight-story building.

Designed by architect Robert Stern, the building opened its doors in 2008 and opened them wide, offering the public a new destination experience in its lobby. A two-thousand-square-foot LED screen projects images so realistic, they appear to be bursting forth from the wall. The company claims the so-called Comcast Experience offers a resolution five hundred times greater

1701 John
F. Kennedy
Boulevard
Philadelphia, PA
19103
www.visitphilly
.com/museums-
attractions/
philadelphia/
comcast-center

than a high-definition television. The screen show runs throughout the day with a variety of content, from views of Philly hot spots to dance and acrobatic performances. During December an on-the-hour holiday spectacular has become a must-see for those taking in the sights of the season. The lobby also features ten life-size figures by sculptor Jonathan Borofsky perched on horizontal poles that rise through the atrium. Directly below the lobby are shops and restaurants offering everything from an on-the-go bite to one of the city's finest restaurants.

The building is striking not only for its size, but also for its sustainable design. It has been called one of the country's greenest buildings. An energy-saving glass curtain wraps around the entire structure, and its water system uses 40 percent less water than a typical office building. Part of the reason is that all restrooms are equipped with waterless urinals, which became something of an issue with the plumbers union during construction.

DOWN THE SHORE

Okay, so it's not Philadelphia. It's not even Pennsylvania, for that matter. But when summer rolls around, nothing says Philly like the Jersey Shore. We don't head to the beach around these parts, we go "down the shore." If you say "down to the shore," you might as well be wearing a T-shirt that reads "I'm not from Philly."

It might be riding the roller coasters in Wildwood or taking in the Victorian charm of Cape May. It could mean the glitz and glamour of the high rollers in Atlantic City or a quiet walk around a Long Beach Island lighthouse. For some families, it's an annual week spent exploring the boardwalk in Ocean City. Whatever the destination, the tides pull Philadelphians down in masses each year to the narrow barrier islands and beach towns, each with its own distinct flavor.

It's not always easy to get down the shore—with traffic piled up to get over the bridges or causeways—but once

the soil gets sandy and gulls start to squawk, it's worth it. Grab a beach tag, claim your spot, dig in the umbrella, and take in the scene: kids digging for crabs, crowds of teens body-surfing, the whistle of the lifeguard when someone strays too far, biplanes pulling banners advertising concerts and boat outings, the bells signaling the arrival of the ice-cream truck.

There are people crabbing off the docks. Fourth of July parades. Shellfish shacks. Miniature golf. Families waiting to cross the main streets with their arms loaded with beach chairs and buckets of sand toys. Bike rentals. Nightly grilling by renters who have met the fishing boats on their return. Sunburned girls buying lotion at the corner market. It's about as classic a beach experience as you can get. And in this case, "beach" is the correct term, because while Philadelphians go down the shore, once we get there, we head to the beach.

EASTERN STATE PENITENTIARY

In the 1820s the section of Philadelphia now known as Fairmount was farm country that seemed worlds away from the bustling new city. What better place to put a prison? Which explains why a huge, hulking, heavily fortified building sits smack in the middle of one of the city's most desirable residential neighborhoods.

Eastern State Penitentiary was revolutionary when it was built at a cost of $780,000—at the time the largest and most expensive building constructed in the United States. It had central heating. It had running water. And it had flushing toilets, which hadn't even made it into the White House yet. What it also had was a design that reflected an entirely new philosophy of how to incarcerate criminals. Its radial footprint of long churchlike halls and individual cells supported the new concept that introspection and isolation would lead to penitence—thus the word "penitentiary."

Prisoners were kept alone in their cells, which were lit by a single skylight seen as the "Eye of God." Each cell had

2124 Fairmount Avenue
Philadelphia, PA
19130
(215) 236-5111
www.eastern
state.org

its own area for the day's one hour of allotted exercise, enclosed by high walls so prisoners couldn't communicate with each other. It was believed that enough time spent alone in thought and reflection would lead to true repentance. Instead, it drove some of the inmates out of their minds. After visiting Eastern State in 1842, Charles Dickens wrote, "I hold this slow and daily tampering with the mysteries of the brain to be immeasurably worse than any torture of the body." By 1913 the approach was abandoned.

Although declared a National Historic Landmark in the 1960s, Eastern State was abandoned in 1971, though saved from demolition. For the past twenty years, it has slowly been brought back to life as a museum and historic site, and now hosts tours and art installations—with a decidedly creepy background. The highlight of the year comes each October when the penitentiary gets all gussied up for Halloween and hosts "Terror Behind the Walls" tours, complete with insane prisoners and no shortage of gruesome goings-on.

FAIRMOUNT PARK

Covering 10 percent of the land in the city, Fairmount Park is Philadelphia's green gem. The name is a bit of a misnomer, because Fairmount Park is actually made up of sixty-three individual parks that collectively form one of the largest urban parks in the world. Straddling both sides of the Schuylkill River, the park also encompasses Wissahickon Creek and its surrounding Wissahickon Valley, which offers miles of hiking trails so beautiful it's hard to believe it's so close to a big city. As far back as 1844, Edgar Allan Poe wrote, "Now the Wissahiccon [sic] is of so remarkable a loveliness that, were it flowing in England, it would be the theme of every bard." It is just as beautiful today.

Fairmount Park is intricately tied to Philadelphia's history. Mills operating on the waters of the Wissahickon were one of the city's first main industries. Taverns and roadhouses dotted the valley at that time. The Valley Green Inn, built in 1850, still operates today on Forbidden Drive, the main trail through the Wissahickon Valley. Scattered throughout the park are a number of historic houses dating to the 1800s.

In 1876 West Fairmount Park was the site of the Centennial International Exhibition, though Memorial Hall is the only major building from the fair still standing. Several locations of note occupy part of the grounds of the exhibition. The Horticulture Center was built on the site of the fair's showcase garden. Its greenhouse and gardens provide a flower fix, while a pavilion designed by woodworker Martin Puryear puts visitors right in the treetops. Close by is Shofuso, a Japanese teahouse and garden, where koi swim in a pond and cherry blossoms welcome spring each year.

One of the best views of the Philadelphia skyline can be had from Fairmount Park's Belmont Plateau. The skyline has changed a bit, but the panorama is the same one taken in by the founding fathers during visits to nearby Belmont Mansion, built in 1743.

THE FLOWER SHOW

Just when you think you can't take the grime and gray of winter for one more minute, along comes the Philadelphia International Flower Show the first week of March every year. It's a badly needed burst of spring—more than ten lush acres overflowing with color and scent and dreams of how gardens would look in a perfect world.

The Flower Show has been lifting the spirits of Philadelphians since 1829, when the Pennsylvania Horticultural Society organized the country's first such event. It has since blossomed into the largest indoor horticultural event in the world, drawing more than 250,000 visitors from around the country and the globe. The fun spills out the doors of the convention center into the city streets, with many restaurants and shops offering discounts. Stores spruce up their window displays with flower-related themes.

Inside the massive exhibition space, there are large-scale, elaborate displays by professional designers, but amateurs and local garden clubs get their due as well. Many a Philadelphia gardener has carefully tended a

*Pennsylvania
Convention
Center
12th and
Arch Streets
Philadelphia, PA
19107
(215) 988-8899
www.theflower
show.com*

beloved plant, hoping to make it into the competitive classes. Each year a specific theme dictates the subject of many of the garden designs and craft competitions. There are pressed-plant creations that qualify as true works of art and beautiful jewelry that incorporates plant materials. Without fail, the longest lines are for the spectacular miniature displays. Visitors can get gardening advice from experts who host demonstrations and lectures. Cooking events are thrown in on the side, and, of course, hundreds of vendors offer unique garden-related items. At the end of each day, the sidewalks, buses, and commuter trains are full of tired but contented people heading home with their hands full of bunches of cheery daffodils or wielding an unruly batch of curly willow.

All proceeds from the Flower Show go to support the Horticultural Society's Philadelphia Green urban-revitalization program, which has helped transform many trash-strewn vacant lots into bountiful community gardens and oases of green throughout the city's neighborhoods.

FRANK FURNESS

Some of the most stunning spaces in and around Philadelphia were the vision of one man—architect Frank Furness. Born in 1839, Furness was a lifelong Philadelphian who designed more than six hundred buildings over the course of his career, the majority of them in his hometown.

Furness was trained in the Gothic Revival and Beaux-Arts traditions, to which he added his own idiosyncratic flair and a sharp eye for detail. It's hard to imagine that during the mid-twentieth century many of Furness's buildings fell victim to the wrecking ball in the name of "progress." However, there are enough fine examples of his style still standing that he continues to leave his mark on the look of Philadelphia.

Many believe Furness's crowning achievement was the Pennsylvania Academy of the Fine Arts at Broad and Cherry Streets, which opened in 1876. The ornate exterior juxtaposes sandstone, pink granite, red brick, and terracotta accented by floral motifs and a bas-relief frieze of famous artists throughout history. As extravagant as

the exterior seems, Furness pulls out all the stops on the interior. The spectacular stair hall leads to gallery space with deep red walls offset with gold floral patterns framed by Gothic arches. Overhead is a vaulted ceiling painted a deep blue, twinkling with silver stars. It's a breathtaking setting for the academy's fine collection.

Another Furness masterpiece is the castlelike Fisher Fine Arts Library on the University of Pennsylvania campus, where brick, terracotta, and multi-floored arches again play a major role in creating the dramatic central space. The reading room, lit from four stories overhead by a skylight, surely offers the best study space in the city.

Furness was a prominent influence on several famous architects, most notably Louis Sullivan, who began his career drafting for Furness's firm. Furness also left his mark on Robert Venturi, who met his wife and partner, Denise Scott Brown, at a rally protesting a ridiculous proposal to tear down the Fisher Library in the 1950s. At the time, Frank Lloyd Wright toured the building, proclaiming it "the work of an artist."

FRANKLIN INSTITUTE

There's a reason the Franklin Institute is the most visited museum in Pennsylvania. Kids love it because it's fun; parents love it because they feel like their kids might actually be learning something. Mission accomplished on both fronts.

The Franklin Institute was hands-on before such a notion became fashionable in museum circles. From the beginning, when the institute was founded in 1824 to honor Benjamin Franklin, it was all about learning through action. When it moved to its current home on the Parkway in 1934, the museum gained more space for interactive exhibits. Today a combination of traveling blockbuster shows and permanent favorites offer a science experience beyond compare.

Some of the most beloved exhibits are actually among the older ones, probably because many parents head to them first with memories of their own childhood visits. A thumping heartbeat coaxes visitors into the Giant Heart, fifteen thousand times a life-size human

222 North
20th Street
Philadelphia, PA
19103
(215) 448-1200
www.fi.edu

heart, where kids scamper up and down its internal passageways following the flow of blood. A three-story Foucault pendulum sways in the museum's marble stairway, while another exhibit offers the opportunity to climb on board a real steam engine. The museum boasts the largest collection of artifacts from the workshop of Orville and Wilbur Wright. And though recently completely renovated, the Fels Planetarium has been exploring the mysteries of the universe since it was built in 1933, making it the nation's second-oldest planetarium. More modern additions like an IMAX theater and the outdoor Science Park only add to the old-time fun.

To enter the museum, visitors walk through the Benjamin Franklin National Memorial, which features a twenty-foot-high marble statue of the man himself. A recent overhaul of the memorial included the addition of a brief multimedia presentation that plays every hour in the rotunda, examining Franklin's numerous contributions and extolling his scientific curiosity.

INDEPENDENCE HALL

Though it can sometimes seem dwarfed by the taller buildings and city bustle that surround it, Independence Hall sits stoically at the core of the history of Philadelphia and the country. It was here the founding fathers signed the Declaration of Independence during the sweltering summer of 1776, and here again eleven years later where representatives of twelve of the new nation's thirteen states (Rhode Island did not attend) gathered to craft the U.S. Constitution.

Construction on what was then known as the Pennsylvania State House began in 1732. It took twenty years to complete; at the time it was the most ambitious public building project in the colonies. Over the years the building went through numerous changes and restorations; the elegant spire wasn't added until 1828. Visitors today can see the Assembly Room, dominated by George Washington's "Rising Sun" chair, just as it looked during the Constitutional Convention. An original draft of the Constitution is on display, as is the inkstand that was used when the Declaration of Independence was signed.

Sixth and Chestnut Streets Philadelphia, PA 19106 (215) 965-2305 www.nps.gov /inde

Standing in these hallowed spaces, it is not hard to be transported back in time and imagine Franklin, Hamilton, Madison, and the rest debating the details of their new democracy. Though George Washington was unanimously elected president of the convention, it is said he contributed little, knowing his opinion would carry much weight.

Throughout the long, hot summer of 1787—the windows of Independence Hall were kept tightly shut, lest passersby eavesdrop on the proceedings—the delegates worked out the finer points of creating a government. Though there was much disagreement—in the end three delegates refused to sign—the results have stood the test of time. Benjamin Franklin had the last word: "There are several parts of this Constitution which I do not at present approve, but I am not sure I shall never approve them. . . . I doubt too whether any other Convention we can obtain, may be able to make a better Constitution. . . . It therefore astonishes me . . . to find this system approaching so near to perfection as it does; and I think it will astonish our enemies."

ITALIAN MARKET

Technically it's known as the "Ninth Street Curb Market"—at least that's what it says on the marker that came with its historical designation. But most people call the open-air market that runs along Ninth Street in South Philadelphia the Italian Market. Even that is deceptive. True, there are plenty of Italian vendors offering fresh pasta, an amazing array of cheeses, and tasty specialties from the homeland, but over the decades the market has taken on a decidedly international flavor.

Ninth Street has been a bustling market since the late 1800s, when Italian immigrants flocked to the neighborhood. Some current shops trace their roots to those early days, when owners lived above their storefronts. Today immigrants continue to settle in the area; recently Vietnamese, Korean, Chinese, and Mexican businesses have set up shop, and a wide range of foreign languages make up part of the sounds of the market. Visitors are also likely to hear a few colorful remarks, as vendors engage in friendly competition for customers.

Ninth Street between Wharton and Fitzwater www.italian marketphilly.org

Cold winter days find sellers and buyers warming their hands over fires built in barrels, while the hot days of summer may be a little more aromatic than most would like. But year-round the market offers a true slice of Philadelphia street life. Most first-time visitors recognize the market as a location featured prominently in Rocky Balboa's training route in the first *Rocky* movie. In the years since the movie was released, things have been cleaned up a bit as the market set its sights on attracting tourists. Still, most people here are locals who have been coming to their favorite shops for years.

For those not inclined to shop and do the cooking themselves, there are plenty of restaurants tucked in between and around the stalls. And it's not just about the food. You can find almost anything in the Italian Market, from high-end housewares to books to clothing; some stalls even offer everything from socks to toiletries to laundry detergent at bargain-basement prices.

LAUREL HILL CEMETERY

Admittedly, it can seem a little creepy. And there are some who grumble that when it comes to having a room with a view, one of Philadelphia's prime real estate locations is wasted on the dead. But there's no denying that Laurel Hill Cemetery, perched on sloping hills in Fairmount Park overlooking the Schuylkill River, is a beautiful place to be—or not be, as the case may be. Many simply admire its towering monuments while driving along the river, while others have taken the time to explore its history—and been richly rewarded for doing so.

Laurel Hill opened in 1836, the result of efforts by a Quaker named John Jay Smith, who was disgusted at being unable to find the grave of his own daughter in an overcrowded city graveyard. From the beginning Laurel Hill was unique in several ways: Smith insisted it be in a picturesque location, that it have no religious affiliation, and that it provide a permanent burial space in a tranquil setting. Until then, it was not uncommon for the dead to be disinterred to make way for

3822 Ridge Avenue
Philadelphia, PA 19132
(215) 228-8200
www.thelaurel
hillcemetery.org

the growing city. The grounds were laid out by Scottish architect John Notman, who conceived of the cemetery as an estate garden and whose tiered design took full advantage of the view of the river. The river was also important in bringing city-dwellers to the cemetery, and by the 1840s steamboats operated frequently to the site. Laurel Hill became not just a refuge for the dead, but a retreat for the living. Weekends found a parade of visitors taking carriage rides and strolls through the grounds, with families picnicking in the fresh air.

A visit to the cemetery today affords the opportunity to take in not only the view, but an astonishing collection of sculptures and architecturally detailed monuments and mausoleums. Laurel Hill is one of the few cemeteries in the nation to be designated a National Historic Landmark. It is also the final resting place of a number of Philadelphia's early power barons, as well as forty Civil War–era generals, including General George Meade, the Union victor at Gettysburg.

LIBERTY BELL

It doesn't get much more iconic than this: the Liberty Bell—the grand lady of them all. There she hangs—all quiet and cracked—the object of adoration and thousands of photographs daily.

Cast in London's Whitechapel Foundry, the bell arrived at what was then known as the Pennsylvania State House in 1753. And what a bell it was—more than two thousand pounds with a forty-four-pound clapper, inscribed with a verse from Leviticus: "Proclaim Liberty throughout all the Land unto all the Inhabitants thereof."

The only problem was that the very first time it rang, that clapper cracked the bell. Two local artisans—John Pass and John Stow—started over, melting down the metal, adding a little copper to make it stronger, and recasting it; actually, they recast it twice. (Thus the "Pass and Stow / Philada / MDCCLIII" inscribed front and center.) It still wasn't perfect, but the bell was installed in the tower of the State House.

Sixth and Chestnut Streets Philadelphia, PA 19106 (800) 537-7676 www .independence visitorcenter.com

The bell rang often in the early days, summoning people for important announcements and events. Though some historians doubt its accuracy, legend has it that its most famous ringing was on July 8, 1776, announcing the first public reading of the Declaration of Independence. When the British occupied Philadelphia in 1777, the bell was whisked away to Allentown and hidden in the floorboards of a church. It returned to chime importantly when Philadelphia assumed its role as the nation's capital. But on Washington's Birthday in 1846, all that happy ringing came to an abrupt end when the crack of all cracks "put it completely out of tune and left it a mere wreck of what it was," as the local paper put it at the time.

It was the adoption of the bell as a symbol by abolitionists, who were the first to dub it the "Liberty Bell," that truly hoisted it to iconic status. The symbolism only increased after the Civil War, when the Liberty Bell was sent on the road, traveling across the country as a sign of unity.

LOVE PARK

It seems only fitting in the City of Brotherly Love that there be a place that's all about love. And so there is—Love Park, which anchors the City Hall end of the Benjamin Franklin Parkway. It's not hard to figure out why Philadelphians call it Love Park, even though its official name is the John F. Kennedy Plaza. It's dominated by one of artist Robert Indiana's *LOVE* sculptures, an iconic image in modern American art if ever there was one. (Another is tucked away on the campus of the University of Pennsylvania.)

Built over a parking garage in 1965, the park was the vision of city planner Edmund Bacon (father to actor Kevin) and architect Vincent Kling, who wanted to create a gateway to the Parkway. Curved granite steps encircle a spouting fountain, whose water can change color to mark special occasions. Indiana's sculpture was installed in 1976 as part of the country's bicentennial festivities, but the artist had it removed two years later after the city couldn't afford to buy it. Riding to the rescue came

16th Street and John F. Kennedy Boulevard

philanthropist and Philadelphia art commissioner Fitz Dixon, who shelled out $35,000 to bring back the *LOVE*.

It hasn't always been hugs and kisses at the park, though. There's still bad blood between the city and the skateboarders. There was just something about the circular steps and the solid granite ledges that turned Love Park into one of the world's premier skateboarding sites in the 1980s and '90s. It drew boarders from around the world, as well as hordes from the city's neighborhoods who just wanted to work on their chops. The city's international skateboarding reputation was largely responsible for Philadelphia being chosen to host the 2001 and 2002 X-Games for extreme sports enthusiasts. But that's where it ended, because in 2002 the city began enforcing a skateboarding ban in public places and spent $800,000 on a remodeling job that spiffed up the ledges and benches in such a way as to end the appeal for boarders. So much for sharing the love.

THE MAIN LINE

The Main Line: three little words that conjure up images of lavish debutante balls, lazy summer afternoons spent sipping lemonade and playing cricket on well-manicured lawns, and cocktails at the country club after a long, hard day on the links. No matter that there's not much truth to those stereotypes anymore; the myth of the Main Line was cast in stone (out of which so many Main Line houses are made) when Katharine Hepburn sashayed her way through *The Philadelphia Story.* The 1940 film starring Hepburn, Cary Grant, and Jimmy Stewart was based on the life of feisty Hope Montgomery Scott, a Main Line socialite whose family's Main Line estate still stands.

The unglamorous truth is that "Main Line" refers to some old railroad tracks. The term grew out of what was known as the Main Line of Public Works of the State of Pennsylvania, which included the construction of the state's first railroad. That eighty-two-mile line ran from Philadelphia through Lancaster to Columbia on the Susquehanna River. When it was being built, the rail line provided the first easy access from Philadelphia to the surrounding countryside, and some of the city's wealthiest residents built estates as weekend retreats. In the late nineteenth century, the railroad encouraged the development of residential communities by building more stations. Up sprang stations in Overbrook, Merion, Narberth, Wynnewood, Ardmore, Haverford, and Bryn Mawr (remembered by generations of Main Liners by the phrase "Old Maids Never Wed And Have Babies"). Now known as the Paoli local, the commuter line actually extends beyond Paoli past Downingtown all the way out to Thorndale.

While the area is still home to some of the region's most exclusive country clubs and elite private schools, it is no longer the bastion of WASP society that it once was. (Fun fact: The man who coined the term "WASP"—for White Anglo-Saxon Protestant—was himself a WASPy Philadelphian.) Though still decidedly upscale, the Main Line is now home to people from a wide variety of religious and ethnic backgrounds.

MEMORIAL HALL

In 1876 about ten million people—approximately 20 percent of the country's population at the time—attended the Centennial International Exhibition in Philadelphia. Only one major building from the exhibition remains—Memorial Hall in Fairmount Park, among the most elegant structures in Philadelphia. Designed by Hermann Schwarzmann, the stately building is topped by an iron and glass dome and a statue of Columbia, which peeks above the trees to greet drivers and rowers in Fairmount Park.

The Beaux-Arts beauty housed the Centennial's art exhibits and later served as the first home of the Philadelphia Museum of Art. In the middle of the last century, however, the building grew tired and lost its luster, serving as a recreation center and ultimately housing only a run-down police station. It closed altogether in 2000, leaving behind crumbling walls and a leaky roof. But the last decade has seen Memorial Hall return to its original

Please Touch Museum at Memorial Hall 4231 Avenue of the Republic Philadelphia, PA 19131 (215) 581-3181 www.pleasetouch museum.org

shine, thanks to the city's Please Touch Museum, which pumped $88 million into a spectacular renovation. In 2008 the children's museum threw open its impressive doors and reveled in the space, more than three times bigger than its previous cramped quarters.

The Please Touch is a children's paradise, full of interactive exhibits. Kids can play croquet with the Queen in Alice's Adventures in Wonderland, get behind the wheel of a real city bus, and play hopscotch on a cloud. The adults will appreciate the whimsical sculptures, especially the forty-foot-high depiction of the Statue of Liberty's arm and torch, specially designed for the space by local artist Leo Sewell and constructed completely out of discarded materials. And everybody thrills at the opportunity to climb aboard the Woodside Park Dentzel carousel, which was built in 1908 for an amusement park nearby but had sat in storage for forty years until the Please Touch brought it back to life.

MOTHER BETHEL AME

In 1797 a simple wood-frame blacksmith shop was erected on a lot near Sixth and Lombard Streets in Philadelphia. Richard Allen, a lay preacher, had purchased the shop for $35, then hired a team of horses to pull it to his lot. Allen, a former slave, had grown fed up that he and other blacks were forced to sit separately in balconies during worship services at the city's churches. From that humble blacksmith shop grew the Mother Bethel African Methodist Episcopal (AME) Church, the foundation of the nation's first black denomination. The ground on which the current Mother Bethel stands remains the oldest piece of land in the country continuously owned by African Americans.

Allen became the church's founding pastor and first bishop. He was already an important figure in the city's black community; he opened a school in 1795 and urged his fellow African Americans to provide public service during the yellow fever outbreak in 1793. He was later instru-

419 South Sixth Street Philadelphia, PA 19147 (215) 925-0616 www.mother bethel.org

mental in recruiting black soldiers during the War of 1812, and his church became an important stop on the Underground Railroad. Among those to speak from Mother Bethel's pulpit were Frederick Douglas and Sojourner Truth.

The current Romanesque Revival church building, designed by architect Edward Hazelhurst, was finished in 1889. Of particular note are the stained-glass windows of religious and Masonic images. Allen and his wife, Sarah, are buried in a crypt in the building's lower level. A small museum contains a wooden pew from the original blacksmith's shop, the original unpolished wood pulpit built by Allen himself, and Allen's personal Bible, believed to have been printed in the 1600s.

The African Methodist Episcopal Church today has more than 2.5 million members. The denomination's symbol depicts a cross and an anvil, harkening back to the church's beginnings in Richard Allen's blacksmith shop.

MUMMERS

In most cities in the civilized world, the major revelry welcoming a new year takes place on New Year's Eve. People gather together, sing and dance, usually drink too much, then crawl into bed in the early morning hours and sleep it off until the football games start. Suffice it to say that this is not how Philadelphia celebrates the New Year.

Meet the Mummers, a Philly tradition that truly has to be experienced to be believed. Grown men—yes, mostly men, mainly blue-collar carpenters, plumbers, electricians, and the like—spend outrageous amounts of time and money every year for the chance to march in the freezing cold in the annual Mummers Parade. They spend untold hours constructing movable scenery and elaborate costumes bedecked with sequins and feathers, then grab their banjos and glockenspiels and hit South Broad Street on New Year's Day to strut their stuff. And strut they do—literally—all the way up to City Hall, where the surprisingly intense judging for cash prizes

Mummers Museum
1100 South Second Street
Philadelphia, PA 19147-5497
(215) 336-3050
www.mummers museum.com

takes place. "Oh Dem Golden Slippers"—the parade's anthem—sounds out loud and clear and often.

The first Mummers Parade was held in Philadelphia on January 1, 1901, to welcome the new century, but the tradition dates back centuries. (The word itself comes from Momus, the Greek god of mockery and satire.) The celebration is now an all-day affair featuring upwards of ten thousand participants, from the clowns of the Comic division to the feathers of the Fancies and the Fancy Brigades to the all-out choreography and controlled chaos of the String Bands. Once the parade winds down, the groups head back to their clubhouses on Second Street—or "Two Street," to those in the know—to continue the celebrations. There's also a Mummers Museum on Two Street, for those who can't make the parade, where visitors can take in the costumes and memorabilia of past parades and even try their hand—or feet, as it were—at the inimitable Mummers strut.

MURALS

It started out as a simple idea: Why not hire graffiti artists to paint murals on the sides of buildings rather than have them cover these urban canvases with unsightly scrawls and tags? From its beginning as part of the city's Anti-Graffiti Network, the hugely successful Mural Arts Program has completed more than three thousand murals across the city's many neighborhoods, making Philadelphia the mural capital of the world.

When the city hired muralist Jane Golden in 1984 to reach out to graffiti artists, they had no idea what they were in for. Golden has turned the program into the largest public art project in the country. But this is not just about painting pretty pictures on public walls. Each mural is a community effort, designed after consulting with neighborhood leaders and residents, resulting in a mural that reflects the culture or concerns of its individual neighborhood. Many are installed next to abandoned lots, which not only beautifies an eyesore but results in stabilizing a community's open spaces. Some feature hometown heroes such

as 76ers legend Julius Erving—Dr. J— while others offer peaceful panoramas on bustling streets.

The Mural Arts Program employs three hundred artists each year and also runs unique educational programs in schools and recreation centers to reach out to three thousand at-risk youth, teaching life skills through creative teamwork. It also works with the prison system to engage current and former inmates in a creative outlet.

The average mural takes about two months to complete and is approximately the size of a row house, though a recent undertaking at the Philadelphia airport is beautifying the walls of parking garages with a fifty-thousand-square-foot mural. One recent installation consists of fifty smaller rooftop murals that constitute one long love letter, and can only be seen in its entirety by riders on the Market Street elevated transit line. Philadelphia's murals have become such an integral part of the city's image that visitors can now take trolley tours through neighborhoods and hear the stories behind the individual works of art.

THE PALESTRA

It's known as the Cathedral of College Basketball, and for many a trip to the Palestra on the University of Pennsylvania campus is a spiritual pilgrimage indeed. The walls echo with the cheers of the frenzied fans that have filled the bleachers since the building opened in 1927. The Palestra is home to Philly's Big 5—Penn, Villanova, Temple, St. Joseph's, and LaSalle—one of the greatest basketball rivalries in college sports. Die-hard fans insist that to attend a game at the Palestra is to see basketball the way it was meant to be played: no glitzy JumboTron screens or fancy scoreboards, no expensive food or skyboxes—just an arena packed with fans filling bleachers so close to the court, they become part of the action itself.

Les Keiter, the voice of the Big 5 during the sixties, said, "I don't think there's a place on earth that is comparable to it." That was back in the days when fans covered the floor with streamers after their team's first basket and slowly unfurled roll-out banners

220 South 32nd Street Philadelphia, PA 19104 (215) 898-6151

in the stands. (The streamers were allowed to make a brief return several years ago to celebrate the Big 5's fiftieth anniversary.)

The history of the Palestra is so compelling that during a recent renovation of the building, parts of the lobby and concourse were turned into what is essentially a museum of Philadelphia basketball. When the floorboards needed to be replaced a few years ago, they were fashioned into picture frames, pens, and cufflinks sold to fans who just had to have a piece of the place. They even made bottle openers that come with a piece of netting from the rims, complete with a certificate of authenticity.

Even though Penn has spent millions fixing up the place, they were smart enough to leave the basics untouched, so the history still pervades. The magic of the Palestra—and the game played on its court—is spelled out on a plaque inside: "To win the game is great. To play the game is greater. But to love the game is the greatest of all."

PHILLIE PHANATIC

In the world of sports, there are mascots and then there are mascots. With absolutely no offense intended to Swoop or Hip-Hop—who perform their duties diligently for the Eagles and the 76ers respectively—it's still the Phillie Phanatic that is nearest and dearest to the hearts of Philly fans. And why not? He's even named after them. He's also the only mascot in the Baseball Hall of Fame.

The Phanatic cruises around Citizens Bank Park on his ATV, thumbing his trumpet of a nose at the umps. His forays into the stands frequently find him trying to swipe some poor guy's girlfriend, sending a tub of popcorn flying after a clumsy trip, or plopping his ample behind on the lap of an unsuspecting fan. Between innings, he fires up his Hot Dog Launcher, sending cooked dogs soaring into the upper decks. The Phanatic also spends a good amount of time atop the Phillies dugout, taunting opposing pitchers—he is a Philly fan, after all.

The Phanatic's major-league debut came on April 25, 1978, in the old Veterans Stadium. The character had been cooked up by the Harrison/Erickson firm in New York, which had ties to Jim Henson's Muppets. That likely accounts for the googly eyes. At the time, Phillies chairman Bill Giles opted to pay $3,900 for the costume alone rather than cough up an additional $1,300 to obtain the copyright as well. Giles later called it the worst decision of his life. Five years later the team paid Harrison/Erickson $250,000 for the copyright to the Phanatic, who was wildly popular from the start.

The team has done a great job of hiring guys who really know how to take that costume for a ride. As was rightly noted in *USA Today,* "From the top of his neon-green head to the tip of his bubble-toed size 20 shoes, the Phillie Phanatic is every inch the best mascot in the business. He's as much Philadelphia as cheesesteaks, the Liberty Bell, and Rocky Balboa."

PSFS BUILDING

The nighttime Philadelphia skyline is dominated by twenty-seven-foot-high neon red letters—P S F S—rising thirty-three stories above street level. The sign was such an integral part of the city skyline that when the building on which it sits was purchased by the Loews Corporation and turned into a high-end hotel, they were smart enough to respond to cries of protest by leaving the signature letters in place and brightly lit. It's said you can see them from twenty miles away on a clear night.

PSFS—the Philadelphia Saving Fund Society—went out of business in 1992, but its headquarters remain an important part of Philadelphia's architectural history. Designed by George Howe and William Lescaze in the early 1930s, the building was the first International-style skyscraper in the United States. It is still considered a masterpiece of early modernist architecture. Revolutionary at the time, the building's design called for simplified, functional architecture without excessive decoration. The T-shaped tower sits

Loews Philadelphia Hotel
1200 Market Street
Philadelphia, PA 19107
(215) 627-1200
www.loewshotels .com/hotels /philadelphia

atop a base covered with polished gray granite; the unusual decision to put the banking hall on the second floor allowed for retail stores at street level.

The building's interior included custom-made Cartier clocks and tubular steel furniture designed specifically for the space. It was also the first building of its size to boast year-round air-conditioning. It wasn't universally loved, however. One critic wrote, "Never has such an ugly building been perpetrated." But architect Robert Stern later wrote, "[PSFS] is a superbly crafted object, refined in its every detail. . . . [It] is that rarest of phenomena of our time, a working monument."

When Loews renovated the building into a hotel, the designers left many of the building's details intact. The lobby is dominated by the original vault door and the bronze ceiling of what used to be the safe-deposit box area. The dramatic main banking room on the second floor was converted into a ballroom.

QUAKERS

Forget the guy on the container of oats. He's got nothing to do with the people who settled Philadelphia in the mid-1600s. Those Quakers, led by William Penn, were the ones responsible for laying the literal and spiritual foundations of Philadelphia.

Quakers are members of the Religious Society of Friends, a faith traced to an Englishman named George Fox and a period of religious upheaval in seventeenth-century England. The religion continues to be practiced around the world in a variety of forms. And even though only a tiny percentage of Philadelphians actually practice the religion, Quaker beliefs and traditions continue to shape the city, even today. Quaker meetinghouses dot communities throughout the area, and Friends schools remain vibrant, well-regarded educational institutions from preschools through distinguished local colleges.

The Quaker faith is founded on four basic tenets, which are referred to as testimonies: peace, equality, integrity, and simplicity. Quakers believe there is "that of God in everyone." Their meetinghouses are simple buildings with no religious ornamentation; rows of wooden pews from all sides face the center. Services are conducted primarily in silence with no music or sermonizing, except when members are moved by "the light" to share a prayer or message. Quaker business decisions are reached through consensus; rather than voting, those attending work to gain a sense of God's will. That can make for some long meetings, but the process results in a decision supported by all.

The Quaker beliefs of religious tolerance and simplicity were at the core of Philadelphia's founding. William Penn envisioned a city where equals could worship freely and govern themselves. These principles drew many bright minds to Philadelphia, and the city prospered. Over the centuries Quakers have been at the forefront of social causes; women were treated and educated equally to men from the start, and Quakers were among the first to call for the abolition of slavery.

READING TERMINAL MARKET

Visitors to the Reading Terminal Market should prepare for sensory overload. Take one giant train shed and fill it with more than eighty stands offering any kind of food you can imagine—dished up with a side of Philly attitude—and the result is about as lively as it gets. It's a crush of tastes, smells, sights, sounds, and, yes, touch—that many say offers the most authentic Philadelphia experience there is.

Established in 1892, Reading Terminal is the country's oldest continuously operating farmers' market. All of the stalls are individually owned—no McDonald's here—and a handful have stayed in the same family for generations. Though almost dealt a knockout blow by the decline of the rail industry and suburban flight, the market found new life in the 1980s and is now run by a nonprofit corporation. It's as busy as ever.

Whatever you want, it's here: traditional farm-fresh Pennsylvania Dutch

12th and Arch Streets Philadelphia, PA 19107 (215) 922-2317 www.reading terminalmarket .org

dishes and homemade jams brought from Lancaster County by Amish families; wide-ranging ethnic options; and, of course, time-honored Philly favorites, with some of the best cheesesteaks, roast pork sandwiches, and hoagies in town. Oprah herself declared Delilah's macaroni and cheese to be the best in the land. Fresh produce, cheese, seafood, poultry, meat, baked goods, and buckets of flowers line the aisles, with a sampling of cookware and craft items thrown in.

A central area for seating is watched over by Philbert, the market's piggy-bank mascot, whose donations go to support local food charities. An upright piano sits among plastic chairs way in the back, and there's almost always someone playing for tips. A revolving group of talented pianists—some highly trained, some just born with the gift—provides a musical backdrop for the sounds of the bustling market.

RITTENHOUSE SQUARE

In its early days Rittenhouse Square was just livestock pasture known as a good spot for disposing of "night soil." It's come a long way, and this urban oasis is now a favorite gathering spot and the center of one of the city's toniest neighborhoods.

The square was one of William Penn's five original public gathering places, then simply called Southwest Square. In the late 1700s brickyards sprang up around the square to take advantage of its clay soil. The name change came in 1825, when the site was renamed to honor David Rittenhouse, known as the finest astronomer of his time. He was also a clockmaker, a friend of Ben Franklin's, and served as the first director of the U.S. Mint.

In the 1850s elegant town houses started to pop up; some still line the small streets in the neighborhood, though most of the space facing the square itself has been given over to high-end condominiums. The surrounding area is home to some of the

18th and Walnut Streets

best restaurants and shopping that Philly has to offer.

The main attraction, however, is still the square itself. In 1913 architect Paul Cret was brought in to design the entrances and a central plaza with a pool, fountain, and elegant stone railings. The open space draws crowds throughout the day, whether they're just cutting across the square, walking their dogs, or taking advantage of the benches to read, have an outdoor lunch, or catch the occasional nap. It's a haven for young children, who are drawn to the lion and goat statues and enjoy using their sidewalk chalk on the walkways, while the moms congregate nearby. Buskers regularly claim prime spots and fill the air with music of all types. Weekends find a variety of annual festivals and art shows. An active community group keeps things in tip-top shape, making sure the square is stocked with flowers in the summer, tree lights over the holidays, and bags for people to pick up after their dogs year-round.

ROCKY

He's an unlikely ambassador for the city, but it's fair to say that Rocky Balboa has done more to make the world aware of Philadelphia than anyone else, living or fictional. It's hard to believe it's been more than three decades since Balboa, in the guise of Sylvester Stallone, first sprinted up the Art Museum's seventy-two steps and into the city's collective identity. Pure South Philly, Rocky can also be credited with the most widely quoted use of the city's signature "Yo." According to the American Film Institute, "Yo, Adrian!" is the eightieth top movie quotation in the history of American cinema.

Filmed for just $1.1 million dollars and shot in under a month, the first *Rocky* movie went on to earn more than $225 million worldwide and won the Oscar for Best Picture in 1976. It also made Sylvester Stallone a star and led to five sequels.

All you have to do to see what a phenomenon Rocky is in Philadelphia is stand at the top of the Art Museum

steps, where at any given time on any given day there is sure to be someone standing with his or her arms thrust skyward in Rocky's triumphant pose. Cue "Gonna Fly Now." There's even a conveniently placed set of footprints to show you just where to stand. Without a doubt, the steps are one of the city's top tourist attractions.

At the base of the steps stands Rocky's iconic image cast in bronze. Stallone commissioned the nine-foot statue, which was installed at the top of the steps for the filming of *Rocky III.* He later donated the statue to the city, but a debate ensued about whether the statue was a legitimate work of art or a movie prop. For a time it was moved to the Sports Complex, where it took up residence outside the Spectrum. After being returned to the top of the steps for cameo appearances in *Rocky V, Mannequin,* and *Philadelphia,* the statue was installed in a compromise location—at the base of what are commonly called the "Rocky steps."

ROW HOUSES

Rows of attached houses are fairly ubiquitous in America's cities, but Philadelphia's row houses stand in a league of their own. For one thing, this is where this urban housing tradition started. You'd never know it to walk down Jeweler's Row on Sansom Street today, but this block of buildings was once called Carstair's Row, named after Thomas Carstair, who designed the homes for developer William Sansom in the early 1800s. It's the oldest stretch of row homes in the country.

"But wait a minute," you may say. "What about Philadelphia's Elfreth's Alley, long touted as the oldest residential street in America?" True, Elfreth's Alley does date to the 1700s, and true, its charming colonial homes do stand in a row. But they have varying heights, widths, and brickwork patterns. The quintessential Philly row houses were built by developers a block at a time in a uniform design. A drive around South

Philadelphia or West Philadelphia or the far Northeast offers block after block of seemingly identical houses attached squarely at the hip. Here lived the families and workers who fueled the city's industrial heyday.

Over time, individual row homes began to take on a character of their own. Some families enclosed a front porch to add more living space inside; others added awnings to their porches. Some owners decided to renovate with aluminum siding; others took a more traditional route. Paint colors began to change, as did roof colors. Still, there is cohesiveness to these neighborhoods. A summer weekend will find any number of streets in a neighborhood closed down with barricades for a block party, smells from the barbecue wafting over kids who are ecstatic they can finally feel free to play in the street, a reminder that any individual block is more than the sum of its parts.

SCRAPPLE

There are those who say a stick-to-your-ribs Philly breakfast isn't complete without scrapple. There are those who wonder why anyone would eat something that tastes like fried dust. And then there are those who say have it your way, just don't ask what's in it, whatever you do. Suffice it to say that this delicacy is made from the parts of a pig that nobody could figure out what else to do with. The dictionary makes it sound a little more palatable: "Cornmeal mush mixed with pork meat and broth, seasoned with onions, spices, herbs, etc., and shaped into loaves and sliced for frying." The name pretty much says it all, as scrapple had to be invented by some scrappy cooks looking for something to do with their kitchen scraps.

Although it actually originated with the Pennsylvania Dutch in Lancaster County, scrapple is a mainstay of the Philly breakfast menu, where it frequently takes the place of sausage. It

comes in blocks, and the experts say the cut is key—the thinner the better. That way it gets crispy on the outside but the inside texture stays soft. Some diner chefs deep-fry it quickly first before putting it on the grill, just for good measure. Some folks like it plain, but those who don't—and they are legion—embellish with just about anything: butter, maple syrup, applesauce, apple butter, eggs, ketchup, or even hot sauce.

After the *New York Times* ran a scrapple recipe in 1872, the letters to the editor poured in for weeks. The detractors chimed in: One called it an "abominable mess," while another said he'd just as soon fry bread in lard and eat it. But one fan termed scrapple "a positive luxury, throwing the Frenchman's pâté de foie gras entirely into the shade." There are those today who still feel the same, and proudly proclaim their loyalty by sporting T-shirts that read "Scrapple: The Other Gray Meat" or "Scrapple: Everything but the Squeal."

SOCIETY HILL

Most visitors to Philadelphia assume that Society Hill got its name because well-heeled society types were drawn to its charming town houses and cobblestone streets. But the community is actually named after the Free Society of Traders, a stock-trading company that invested in developing William Penn's new city in the late 1600s and early 1700s.

It wasn't that long ago that affluent Society Hill was actually considered a very undesirable place to live. As the city expanded westward throughout the nineteenth century, the neighborhood lost its appeal; many houses were left to deteriorate, and markets and businesses boarded up. That all changed in the 1950s, with the creation of the Independence National Historic Park. City, state, and federal governments joined forces in one of the first redevelopment programs aimed at preserving historic buildings in the adjoining neighborhood. At the same time, architect I. M. Pei was hired to design the Society Hill Towers. Some objected to the size of Pei's development, but the influx of residents helped stabilize the commu-

Bounded by Front, Eighth, Walnut, and Lombard Streets

nity. Today the neighborhood is said to contain the largest concentration of original eighteenth- and nineteenth-century architecture in the country.

Of special note are Society Hill's religious institutions. Tucked in a small alley is charming Old St. Joseph's Church (321 Willings Alley), the oldest Catholic church in Philadelphia. St. Peter's Episcopal Church (313 Pine St.) dates to 1761 but remains largely unchanged today, with its high-backed pews and the pulpit and the altar at opposite ends of the sanctuary. Just across the street from St. Peter's graveyard lies Old Pine Presbyterian Church (412 Pine St.), which was used as a hospital by British troops during the Revolutionary War. The Society Hill Synagogue (418 Spruce St.) dates to 1829, when it was designed as a Baptist church by one of the architects of the U.S. Capitol in Washington, D.C.

Also in Society Hill is the wordy Philadelphia Contributionship for the Insurance of Houses from Loss by Fire (212 South Fourth St.), the nation's oldest fire insurance company, which was founded by Ben Franklin in 1752.

SOFT PRETZELS

The best food you can get in Philadelphia is sold on street corners. Ah, the soft pretzel . . . a staple of the Philly diet.

For those whose entire pretzel experience has come from a grocery store bag, the soft pretzel can be a revelation. Large and chewy, it affords no crunch. Sprinkled with salt and topped with mounds of mustard, it's the perfect midafternoon snack picked up from a corner store or a street vendor. Or now you can buy them by the box, since a onetime Philly pretzel hawker founded a line of retail shops known as—what else?—the Philly Soft Pretzel Factory.

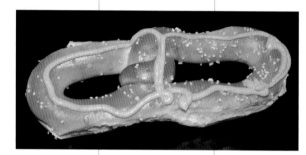

There are a few finer points of soft pretzels that are worth keeping in mind: Don't buy them wrapped in plastic; they'll either be soggy or stale. The paper bag is the conveyance of choice. A good soft pretzel should be topped with coarse salt, but beware if the top looks moist—that means the salt has drawn water out of the dough, so it's probably been sitting around too long. And don't wander off from the vendor until the appropriate amount of mustard has been squirted on the pretzel.

Legend has it that the pretzel is the world's oldest snack food, invented by an Italian monk in the sixth century as a reward for church-going children. The word "pretzel" is said to come from the Latin *pretzola,* or "little reward." A further religious association: Some say the shape of the common pretzel represents arms crossed in prayer, with the empty spaces created standing for the holy Trinity. In modern-day Philly, pretzels aren't quite so hole-y. Most come out of the oven squished together in a long slab. Buy 'em by the bunch for the best price. And buy 'em we do—word is that your typical Philadelphian consumes twelve times more pretzels than the national average.

SOUTH PHILLY

It may be hard to imagine how a huge section of a city could in and of itself be considered iconic, but South Philly pulls it off. Of course, it's really many neighborhoods coming together to create one giant neighborhood that brings together some of the city's most colorful stereotypes.

To begin with, South Philly is Rocky turf. These are the streets he ran through, and his apartment was on Tusculum Street. (South Philly will also give you some of the best street names in a city with no shortage of them. Passyunk and Moyamensing are biggies, for starters.) This is a place that embraces its ethnic flavors. Long a bastion of Italian heritage, some of the city's classic Italian restaurants are located near the Italian Market. Don't order pasta with tomato sauce—it's "red gravy" here.

South Philly is also Mummers land. In the largely Irish neighborhoods surrounding South Second Street—"Two Street" to locals—Mummers clubhouses abound. But while Italians and Irish once dominated, immigrants from many other nationalities now call South Philly home.

Family life is sacrosanct. Many

of these families have lived in the same row houses for generations. And though some neighborhoods have seen increased gentrification along with an influx of more upscale residents and restaurants, the street life remains vibrant. The shoe-throwers in South Philly seem to be particularly abundant and adept at hurling their tied-together discarded sneakers over utility wires.

Parking your car is an art unto itself in South Philly. Spaces are carefully guarded with folding chairs and trashcans, particularly after snowstorms. And it's hard to imagine many other cities where you can get away with parking your car in the middle of the street. But in Philly, once South Broad Street leaves Center City traffic behind, the median fills with a line of parked cars, the Parking Authority having long ago given up on enforcing whatever rules cover such things.

Broad Street takes you to another South Philly landmark—the Sports Complex—the epicenter of Philadelphia's sports scene. Rising from the surrounding parking lots are the homes of all the city's major sports teams.

SOUTH STREET

Dubbed "the hippest street in town" in a 1963 song by the Orlons, South Street still likes to think of itself that way. The song claimed South Street was "where all the hippies meet," though today there are plenty of tourists thrown into the mix. Still, it's a colorful mix of commerce and creativity, with plenty of culinary opportunities to boot.

For much of its history, the South Street area was known primarily as Philadelphia's garment district; that tradition lives on in the stores that line Fourth Street to Catharine Street, known as "Fabric Row." But in the 1950s the threat of a crosstown expressway proposed for the neighborhood sent property values plummeting, and the arts community took advantage of the low rents. Though the expressway was never built, the area developed as the center of the city's counterculture community.

There's still an active live music scene in the area, thanks to several performance venues. A number of restaurants line the street, offering a wide variety of international flavors, but many Philadelphians insist the best food to be had is at Jim's Steaks,

South Street between Front and 11th www.southstreet .com

a perennial contender in the "Best Cheesesteak" contests. Shopping ranges from some of the best shoe stores in town to the more offbeat, such as punk rock headquarters Crash, Bang, Boom and the always-popular Condom Kingdom. One favorite shopping stop is Eye's Gallery, a unique collection of folk art and crafts from around the world. The storefront of Eye's features one of the signature works of Philadelphia mosaic artist Isaiah Zagar, whose wife, Julia, runs the gallery.

Zagar's mosaics show up on the walls and sidewalks up and down South Street, but for the ultimate experience, a trip to the Magic Gardens is in order (1022-24 South St., www.philadelphias magicgardens.org). Zagar started creating his out-of-this-world labyrinth in the 1990s, combining cement, bottles, mirrors, pieces of ceramic, bicycle spokes, and other found objects into a huge indoor/outdoor gallery/sculpture/ maze concoction. Threatened with demolition in 2004 when the lot was sold, the gardens were saved after a public outcry brought a flood of community support and donations.

THE SPORTS FAN

Pick your favorite line. Pete Rose: "Some of these people would boo the crack in the Liberty Bell." Bob Uecker: "You know what they do when the game's rained out? They go to the airport and boo landings." Onetime Phillies coach Jim Fregosi: "The fans in Philly— they're like an extra coach. If they see a guy not running out a grounder, they'll boo the hell out of him. The coach doesn't have to say a thing."

Some use the word "obnoxious" to describe Philadelphia sports fans. In Philly, they prefer "passionate." They think it's gotten a little old, this persistent insistence that Philadelphia sports fans are the most rowdy, rude fans out there.

Granted, the fans can be a little vocal about their displeasure at their teams' performances and not particularly welcoming to visiting teams. Granted, the city decided to open an "Eagles Court" right in the stadium so overly raucous fans can be arrested, tried, and sentenced without leaving the building. Granted, there's just a teeny bit of truth in the story about booing Santa Claus. But it was an inebriated, skinny Santa wannabe who was called into action during halftime of an Eagles game when the real Santa didn't show up. Plus, it was more than forty years ago, so some say it's time to get over it.

What is undeniable is that Philadelphia fans love their sports teams and remain fiercely loyal in the face of years of bitter disappointments. They still rip up bedsheets to make homemade signs. They still come to games dressed in full team regalia. They still show up at the stadium in droves, even when their teams are losing, which they do a lot. Case in point: The Phillies reached a dubious milestone in 2007 when they became the only professional franchise to lose more than ten thousand games. But the following year they put that statistic to bed by winning the World Series. More than two million loyal fans turned out on a weekday to cheer their champions in a parade down South Broad Street.

TASTYKAKES

Butterscotch Krimpets. Koffee Kake Juniors. Peanut Butter Kandy Kakes. Cream Filled Buttercream Cupcakes. It reads like a dream dessert menu for every Philadelphia kid.

Tastykakes—to outsiders, they may seem like any other packaged pastry. But not in Philadelphia, where Tastykakes belong on the food pedestal right along with the cheesesteak. And it's been that way for almost a century. The Tastykake Baking Company was founded in 1914 by Philip Baur, a baker, and Herbert Morris, an egg salesman (and some would say spelling dropouts). The legend has it that Morris's wife was called upon to try the first samples and deemed them "tasty."

The idea was to deliver pre-wrapped, freshly baked goods to the corner store, and it worked. Morris sold $28 worth the first day. The company now boasts gross annual sales of more than $280 million. That's a lot of lunch boxes. And although locals used to have to pack their own when they traveled,

Tastykakes are now sold around the country, where they are scooped up by hungry, homesick Philadelphians.

For decades Tastykakes have been a staple of the Philadelphia sports scene. Hockey season finds Flyers announcers shouting, "He shoots, he scores—for a case of Tastykakes!" And the company has long been a sponsor of the Phillies; at home games, legendary broadcaster Harry Kalas would religiously announce the arrival in the booth of that day's box of Tastykakes.

Keenly aware of its special place in the hearts of Philadelphians, the company plays to the hometown crowd. Its Web site offers a list of tasty trivia. Who knew that it would take 30,412,800 Butterscotch Krimpets to build a three-foot-wide Krimpet sidewalk from Center City to Atlantic City? Or that, if you were so inclined, it would require 172,800 Tastykake Juniors to cover the Flyers' ice rink. You learn something new every day.

VALLEY FORGE

It sometimes seems as though Valley Forge National Historical Park is just a great place to jog or the perfect destination for a weekend bike ride. But if you take a moment to reflect, particularly on a cold winter day, there is a palpable sense of history here and these 3,600 acres feel like hallowed ground.

Some with only a cursory knowledge of American history assume Valley Forge was the site of a major battle during the Revolutionary War. True enough, but no shots were fired. It was here that George Washington and his Continental army hunkered down during the winter of 1778. Having lost control of Philadelphia to the British, the army needed a place to regroup and continue training. With winter closing in, Washington chose a location twenty miles northwest of the city, close enough to keep pressure on the British, but far enough away to provide protection against surprise attacks. Just before Christmas 1777, the troops set up camp and went to work building wooden huts, miles of trenches, and five earthen forts.

Twenty miles northwest of Center City (610) 783-1077 www.nps.gov /vafo

The winter was brutally cold; supplies and food were scarce. But it was actually disease that brought the most suffering. Two thousand soldiers died that winter, most of flu, typhus, typhoid, or dysentery. In a letter to governor George Clinton on February 16, 1778, Washington outlined the deprivation but stated, "Naked and starving as they are, we cannot enough admire the incomparable patience and fidelity of the soldiery." The troops persevered, and a former Prussian officer, Baron Friedrich Wilhelm Augustus von Steuben, arrived to help Washington develop an intense training regimen. The results were apparent when Washington's men soundly defeated the British at the Battle of Monmouth in New Jersey on June 28, after which Washington was able to say the war was going well.

Today the park is dotted with statues, re-created log huts, rows of cannons, and fortifications. A welcome center displays artifacts, Washington's headquarters are open for tours, and a memorial arch designed by Paul Philippe Cret honors those who served during that miserable winter.

WANAMAKER'S

Okay—so it's a Macy's now. But the fact is, for most longtime Philadelphians, the department store at 13th and Market Streets is, was, and always will be Wanamaker's.

For decades this was the ultimate shopping experience, worth getting dressed up for, especially if you could dine in the fancy Crystal Tea Room. Elegance was all around. Founder John Wanamaker provided Philadelphia with two lasting treasures when he imported an organ and an eagle from the 1904 Saint Louis World's Fair. The 2,500-pound bronze eagle sculpture was placed in the Grand Court of his then-new store, where it still stands today. For generations of Philadelphians trying to meet up with friends in Center City, the coordination has been simple: "Meet me at the Eagle." It's a tried-and-true gathering place.

The amazing organ dominates the Grand Court and its five-story atrium. It took thirteen freight cars to bring the organ from Saint Louis to Philadelphia, and two years before it was fully installed in the store. Still not satisfied, Wanamaker hired his own

13th and Market Streets
Philadelphia, PA 19107
(215) 241-9000

organ builders and expanded the organ several times over the years so that its music would adequately fill the cavernous space. Today it is the world's largest pipe organ still in use, with 28,482 pipes. Daily concerts are held at lunchtime and again in the late afternoon or early evening.

The Grand Court becomes even grander during the holidays, when the sights and sounds of the Christmas Light Show return every hour on the hour, just as they have every year since 1956. The show is a barrage of sixty-five thousand blinking lights and blaring holiday music that is refreshingly old-fashioned. No computer animation here—just Frosty and Rudolph and the awkward Nutcracker ballerinas.

Macy's deserves credit for saving another favorite Philly holiday tradition. In 2006, when the curtain came down for rival Strawbridge's, Macy's rode to the rescue and saved the Dickens Village. Here, visitors wander cobblestone pathways while animated figures reenact twenty-six memorable scenes from Dickens's classic *A Christmas Carol*.

WATER ICE

Nothing says summer in Philadelphia like an early evening trip to the water ice place. It's hot and it's been a long day and nothing else will do.

And, yes, we've heard it all before about how the term "water ice" doesn't make any sense. You can call it "Italian ice" if you want, but in Philly it is water ice.

This is not your average snow cone or shaved ice. With water ice, it's all about the texture and the temperature. Not too frozen, not too watery, but smooth, slushy, slurpable, and sweet. Of course, there's the hotly debated question about whether small bits of fruit are acceptable. It's allowed, on occasion, to mix in some frozen custard for gelati. But for the purists, it's still pretty simple—lemon or cherry or mango ice in a paper cup. Add spoon and smile.

Everyone has his or her favorite water ice places, and people are known to travel. Some connoisseurs say the best are those that offer only a handful of flavor choices. Others prefer the wide variety of choices at Rita's—a chain that's trying to take the local craze national. A highlight of the year comes on the first day of spring, when Rita's offers free handouts. The lines are long, but it's worth the wait for that first taste of the season.

But to truly enjoy water ice, you have to wait until the middle of the summer when it's really hot and humid. If you eat dinner on the early side, you can get your water ice, hang out on the stoop with the neighbors for a while, and have just enough time to settle in before the Phillies game starts.

THE WATER WORKS

Three of Philadelphia's most iconic images compete for attention along one short stretch of the banks of the Schuylkill River: the imposing Art Museum, the charming houses of Boathouse Row, and the classic columns of the Fairmount Water Works. Once the source of the city's water supply, the cluster of waterworks buildings now houses an upscale restaurant and an interesting hands-on interpretive center that explores the history and engineering of the city's early water infrastructure.

In the early 1800s Philadelphia desperately needed a new reliable source of clean water for its growing population. As designed by Frederick Graff, first steam engines and later giant paddle wheels pumped water out of the river into a reservoir at the top of the hill, the original "faire mount," where the Art Museum now stands so proudly. Wooden water mains carried the water from the reservoir throughout the surrounding area. At the time it was the most sophisticated water system in the world. But it wasn't just functional—it

Water Works Drive and Kelly Drive Philadelphia, PA 19130 (215) 685-0723 www.fairmount waterworks.org

was beautiful as well, with the classic architecture complemented by sculptures and manicured gardens, and it grew to become a major tourist attraction. It was so popular that in 1835 the engine house that originally housed the steam engines was refashioned into a restaurant to serve the throngs. There diners could look out on the boats that took visitors on river outings.

Early in the twentieth century, with the waters of the Schuylkill increasingly polluted, the mill house was turned into an aquarium. By the 1960s, however, the complex was abandoned and left to deteriorate. In just the past decade, the Water Works has been renovated and shines once more. A restaurant once again fills the engine house, and a former pumping station now houses the interpretive center, where visitors can learn more about the environmental impact of human activity on water quality. In one display a touch of a button creates a downpour then follows the water through watersheds; another puts visitors at the controls of a helicopter cruising the Delaware River.

THE ZOO

One of the best things Philadelphia did before anywhere else in the country got around to it was create a zoo. The Philadelphia Zoological Garden was chartered in 1859, though the Civil War pushed the opening back until 1874. But once a forty-two-acre site in Fairmount Park was selected and an architect was shipped off to London to study the zoo there, things took off. On opening day there were just a few hundred animals; today the zoo is home to more than 1,300 animals and over 300 different species and subspecies. Among the other national firsts it acquired along the way was the first zoo laboratory and the first children's zoo.

It's no accident the zoo is formally called a "zoological garden," as the landscaping and horticultural selections originally got as much attention as the animals. Designed as a Victorian garden, the grounds now contain over five hundred plant species to complement their animal counterparts. There

34th Street and Girard Avenue Philadelphia, PA 19104 (215) 243-1100 www.phillyzoo .org

are architectural gems as well, including gatehouses designed by Frank Furness and "Solitude," a charming neoclassical house originally built as a country home for William Penn's grandson.

For the first fifty years after its opening, getting into the zoo cost 25 cents for adults and 10 cents for children. It's a darn sight more than that now, but there's a lot more to see and do. Recent upgrades include a lush new aviary and new digs for the big cats, where the tigers and lions revel in naturalistic settings. A favorite stop for kids of all ages is the Treehouse, designed by noted Philadelphia architects Venturi, Scott Brown and Associates. Inside the Treehouse, visitors get to experience things from an animal's perspective in several oversize habitats and can climb up the inside of a life-size, four-story rain forest tree. Paddling around Bird Lake in a Victorian swan boat is a favorite childhood memory of many Philadelphians.

PHOTO CREDITS

ABOUT THE AUTHOR

Karen Ivory is a writer living in Philadelphia. A former journalist, she is also the author of *Philadelphia: Off the Beaten Path* and *Pennsylvania Disasters: True Stories of Tragedy and Survival*.